AF270381

AIR JORDAN

KENNY ABDO

Fly!
An Imprint of Abdo Zoom
abdobooks.com

abdobooks.com

Published by Abdo Zoom, a division of ABDO, P.O. Box 398166, Minneapolis, Minnesota 55439. Copyright © 2025 by Abdo Consulting Group, Inc. International copyrights reserved in all countries. No part of this book may be reproduced in any form without written permission from the publisher. Fly!™ is a trademark and logo of Abdo Zoom.

Printed in the United States of America, North Mankato, Minnesota.
102024
012025

Photo Credits: Alamy, AP Images, Everett Collection, Getty Images, Shutterstock
Production Contributors: Kenny Abdo, Jennie Forsberg, Grace Hansen
Design Contributors: Candice Keimig, Neil Klinepier, Laura Graphenteen

Library of Congress Control Number: 2024936557

Publisher's Cataloging-in-Publication Data

Names: Abdo, Kenny, author.
Title: Air Jordan / by Kenny Abdo
Description: Minneapolis, Minnesota : Abdo Zoom, 2025 | Series: Sneakerheads |
    Includes online resources and index.
Identifiers: ISBN 9781098287443 (lib. bdg.) | ISBN 9781098288143 (ebook) |
    ISBN 9781098288495 (Read-to-me ebook)
Subjects: LCSH: Sneakers--Juvenile literature. | Shoes--Juvenile literature. |
    Fashion--Social aspects--Juvenile literature. | Nike (Firm)--Juvenile literature.
Classification: DDC 391.413--dc23

TABLE OF CONTENTS

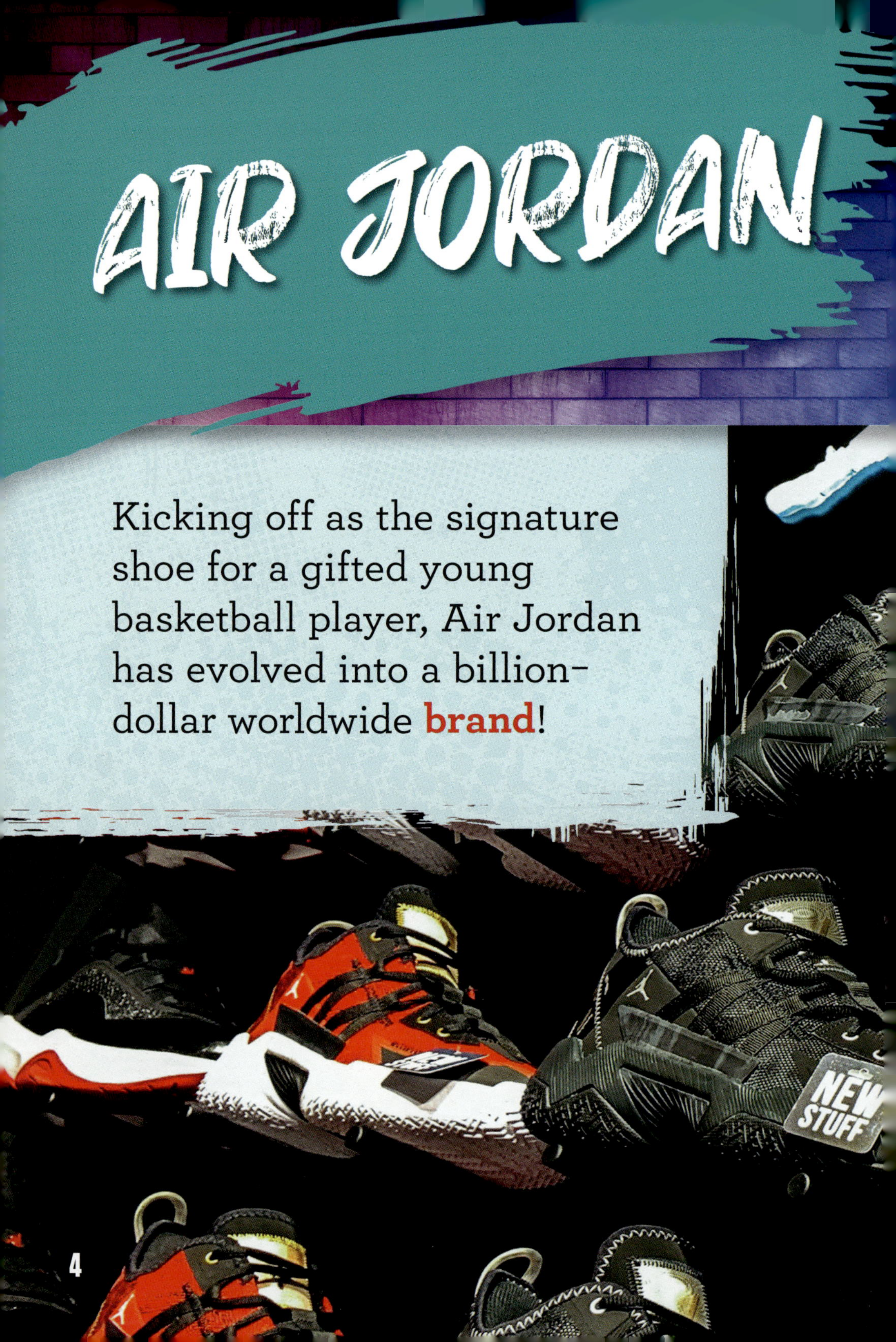

AIR JORDAN

Kicking off as the signature shoe for a gifted young basketball player, Air Jordan has evolved into a billion-dollar worldwide **brand**!

From **hypebeasts** to everyday folk, Air Jordan's have remained outside of the box since their **debut** in 1985!

THE OGs

NBA **rookie** Michael Jordan was approached by many shoe companies. Jordan was not interested in putting his name on shoes that already existed. Nike stepped in and offered to make a shoe just for him.

Designers Peter Moore, Tinker Hatfield, and Bruce Kilgore went to work. They needed a logo that stood out. Nike did a photo shoot with Jordan doing impressive dunks. Finally, the **iconic** sneaker had an iconic logo. It was called the Jumpman.

THE KICKS

Jordan and the shoes hit the court in 1985. However, the shoes violated the NBA's uniform policy. Jordan was hit with a $5,000 **fine** for each game that he wore them. Nike happily paid the fines. And Jordan rocked the shoes in a season that earned him a **Rookie** of the Year award.

The Air Jordan II **debuted** in 1986. The hype for the player and the shoe grew. The AJII were made in Italy with faux lizard skin. They were considered the first luxury basketball shoe by sneakerheads.

JORDAN

Released worldwide in 1989, the Air Jordan IV was the first of its kind. Sneakerheads could lace the shoe up in 18 different patterns. This allowed people to put their own spin on the kicks!

Jordan hit his famous "Last Shot" in 1998. It was his sixth and final **championship**. Jordan **clinched** it while wearing his Air Jordan XIVs. It was the last model he wore as a Chicago Bull.

Air Jordans walked off the court and into pop culture. Rappers, actors, and other celebrities championed the shoes. Air Jordans became a fashion statement.

MADE IN CHINA
FABRIQUE EN CHINE
HECHO EN CHINA
Off-White™ for NiKE
"AIR JORDAN 1"
Beaverton, Oregon USA
C. 1985

Many successful **collaborations** helped grow the **brand**. Collabs with Off-White, Supreme, and Travis Scott were instant hits. Sneakerheads and collectors alike needed the exclusive shoes!

AIR
24

Air Jordans can be spotted in many TV shows and movies. In 2023, the film *Air* was released. The movie starred Matt Damon, Ben Affleck, and Viola Davis. *Air* followed the historic making of the sneaker!

THE RESTOCK

Modern Air Jordan models continue to sellout. Though, some collectors still want a piece of history. In 2023, a pair of AJ XIIIs that had been worn by Jordan during the 1998 NBA **Finals** were **auctioned** off for $2 million!

Even though Michael Jordan retired from the NBA more than 20 years ago, Air Jordans have made anyone who has worn them feel like they could fly!

GLOSSARY

auction – a sale at which goods are sold to the highest bidder.

brand – a name, design, or symbol that separates one product from another.

championship – a game held to find a first-place winner.

clinch – to confirm a win.

collaborate – to work with another person or group to do something or reach a goal.

debut – a first appearance.

Finals – in the NBA, the annual championship series.

fine – a fee paid when a rule is broken.

hypebeast – someone who follows trends in fashion, mainly with streetwear.

iconic – widely known or easily recognized.

rookie – a first-year player in a professional sport.

ONLINE RESOURCES

To learn more about Air Jordan, please visit **abdobooklinks.com** or scan this QR code. These links are routinely monitored and updated to provide the most current information available.

INDEX